What I Do

Healthy Living

We can stay healthy.

We can exercise,

to stay healthy.

We can exercise,

to stay strong.

Here are some ways you can exercise.

I am running.

Running is exercise.

We are dancing.

Dancing is exercise.

We are swimming.

Swimming is exercise.

Swimming will help us,

to stay healthy.

I am roller blading.

Roller blading is exercise.

Roller blading will help us,
to stay healthy.

15

Come on!

Let's all exercise.